Where Dead Things Grow

Jade Davis-Brown
Where Dead Things Grow

All rights reserved
Copyright © 2022 by Jade Davis-Brown

No part of this publication may be reproduced, distributed, or transmitted in any form or by any means, including photocopying, recording, or other electronic or mechanical methods, without the prior written permission of the publisher, except in the case of brief quotations embodied in critical reviews and certain other noncommercial uses permitted by copyright law.

Published by BooxAi

ISBN: 978-965-577-969-1

Where Dead Things Grow

Jade Davis-Brown

To my father, for fiercely loving your darkness, my mother, I love the way you live for the light,
and my twin sister for finding our way through the grey...
without her, this book wouldn't exist.

Thank you to those special souls (you know who you are) that have always been there for me.
I hope my words can bring love to you who are holding this book in your hands.

Jade Davis-Brown

Blooming in the woes,
I have never stopped growing
where the dead things grow.

What is love,
but in thy heart which
shakes the freedom
from our veins.

What fate that I have crossed,
that fair existence gives,
forsaken had I lost,
the death that I once lived.

Follow me down the lane that fades,
like blossoms wilting, to learn my name.
You will not find the same path,
it scatters in many places,
homes without walls and men without faces.
I have found my way...never would have if I stayed.

> The geese fly above
> heading off with second chances
> on their wings.
> I want to be where they fly.

Sometimes, all I need is the air that I breathe
and to love you.

A hug shall find us.
And when it does.
I will embrace it.

> You joined the winged,
> protected by the cover of his night.
> You shall not be forgotten oh marvelous one.
> Hold on to my love and let your pain take flight.

I've lived thousands of lifetimes in this one life.
I cannot comprehend
the beginning to the end,
but I can contend,
that it will bring me back to you.

I never wanted
this world to accept me.
I just wanted
to be able to accept me in this world.

Let there be old souls,
leaping through time just to find,
my primeval heart.

With a thread of faith,
I will stitch you together,
patch you up again.

I'm sorry self
for putting you
through unnecessary hell,
so that I could walk through
fires even when I knew
it would burn.

Coming from a place of happiness
I never knew what freedom was,
what real living is
until I entered an inner sense
of not belonging to the world,
but belonging to myself.
Even if I rise and fall,
it is by the feet
that keep me moving.
This will be the
life that I lead.
As long as it is mine,
it is still worth choosing.

Beneath my surface,
you will not find a soul that claims to be whole.
An array of sorts combined with all the parts that have
canvased in to one.

Why do I carry you up in my heart
and in my mind
when you let me down all the time.

I live in the light,
but came from the night.

I am most at
home in
the unknown.

There are some wounds that cannot heal.
Unsurfaced piles of lingering pain.
Those are the ones that will kill me.

Meet me above the covers
and I will show you how to love
with all of your senses.

A black heart parted my night sky
taking all of my pain with those golden eyes.
An extension of my soul,
that mended me whole.
Of earth and sky, this divine of mine.

I faced my demons head on.
They stand behind me now.

I have bled with wounded monsters,
who have sunk teeth for me,
for they know it is them that I see.
With eyes of unhallowed kindness.

In true form,
you are the
rarest of love.

I held him once,
his wild perfection,
but an untamed heart will always let go.

Evolving from darkness,
the only light I ever knew was you.
Though dust has taken its toll,
you've watered my soul
and are the reason that I grew...

Tiny fragments of you,
still cling to my mind,
closing over my heart,
like an overgrown vine.
They spark and they speck,
may ye never forget,
all the moments we lived,
as one in this life.

When your light goes down,
I'll love you in ways
only darkness has found...

He wore the wild outside
that burned like an
Arabian sunset.

I once glowed with a certain kind of bright,
because I was in the presence of your star.
But that's the thing about stars.
You cannot keep one for too long.
It belongs to the skies, and we are meant to love them,
forever from afar…

I can live
without you, but
I'd rather be
infinitely yours.

Into the darkness I go,
tempered by your bliss.
Unafraid to leave the light,
forever to be missed.

Lay with me music man
and I will let you play with
my heartstrings.

I want brown feathers,
how blessed the dull peaks
that blend together.
Humble, happy, full of bliss.
Strip this glitz upon my face.
Wipe away all glamour with haste.
I do not wish to stand out alone.
I want to blend in,
where the normal ones roam.

How far I've travelled through winters frost,
that's bitten me with perils lost,
to keep me from knowing any warmth at all cost.
Yet still I welcome thy bitter cold winds,
for their outmatched by the sins I've lived in,
and they will not freeze me away from my win.

How can echoes stir a loudness that maddens any silence?
I search these empty halls,
hoping to find you occupying this space.
There are no remnants of your grander.
Only sadness in its place.

The danger of being in love
is being alive
and watching
our love die.

I can't give you words that come from my head,
but I will give you the words of my soul.

Oh forgotten love, I want to burn in your arms so that you can feel my heat transcend.
Oh forgotten love, anything to singe in your skin, so that you will remember me once again.
Let me scar and stain all the pain you have left behind to be your keeper.
And as I burn deeper, let me remind you of what true love really is.
A place where two hearts live.

Bring me peace to this soul, bring me heroes all brave.
Let us offer them healing, it is our turn to save.

> I have entered this earth to give
> everything my soul will allow
> until my time is done.
> Of sky of earth, I will become.
> Then on to anew around the sun.

> Once broken, you can still live
> in a million broken pieces,
> for there is more of you to give...
> more of you to live.

I am certain
that you have
lived such lives
that only Kings
were made for.

> I need to see the sky and stars
> to remind me you exist afar.

Still searching for you, after all of these years.
If I am to reach you, one thing is clear.
You are not of this world, I will not find you here.
Out of the sky, the messengers appear.
Their darkness engulfs me, the closer they near.
Haunting feathers of endless crows whisk me to a place unknown.
As they follow your call. I do not see you anywhere.
I am left standing there, surrounded by them all.
Beguiling back at me, their black eyes watching my every move.
They will not let me pass, until my love, I can prove.
They are the keepers, it is not for me to choose.
I have lost you once already and this time I can't lose.
I begged them to show me, the way to your being.
But they wait for approval, of what I will be seeing.
This life has left me, long ago, I said. I will honor him still, until I am dead.
Their flock grows in size, ready to take me alive.
Mighty wings flap, creating a storm meant for sending me back.
Back where I came, without you again.
I grab on to a nearby weeping willow, and hold on from the scorn.
They will not send me off to the hells of forlorn.
The mighty willows sway, while I yell, I am here to stay.

I begin to wail as the trees of my sorrow, helps me to prevail.
In a flash the crowd of crows grows silent, so I let go of the tree.
My will was not bent, I am ready to see.
Have they found you I asked. Now the old willows begin to sing.
The crows part from their stay and make way for their King.
Stepping out from the darkness, a tall shadow is free.
I have found you at last. Maybe you have found me.
We embrace among the crows who gave me back everything I ever had.
Their ruler, their King, is once again my own dad.

Life is what you can handle
so get a grip.

I don't need just someone.
No, someone would never do.
The only one I ever need,
is the one and only you.

I would trade my light
To make sure that you can fly
Away from the night.

Drifting on the waves of silence, abandoned in your wake.
Stranded by confusing madness, no raft to keep me safe.
The barren salt, it stings my eyes, be it from water or from me.
I'll never see the land again,
you've left me to the sea.

Here I am unimagining myself to fit into your image.
There you are imagining yourself with another.
If only we could imagine each other.

If I am to live without your love,
then be not a second more.
For what else was I born to give?
I have died within your lore.

If I have but one life to live,
let it be within your lifetime.

There is a place that exists only for you.
It is somewhere that I have never been,
but only where you can take me.

I wither like the dying leaves,
of muted tones upon the breeze.
The bits of sun that I have saved,
have gone with the cooling autumn fades.
How fair is love, that's never made,
when it takes thy heart to an early grave.

Be gracious even if they do not deserve your grace.
It will take you places.

Yours is the beauty
that I cannot resist
and don't want to miss.

Am I worthy of your love,
even when I have crossed all barriers
to bring you the stars?
Am I worthy of myself, even if I would have
changed the whole world for you?

You may
have walked away,
but you still manage
to walk all over my heart.

It's not enough to be loved,
unless the world has a place
for our hearts.

While you stay grounded,
I am left there hovering,
waiting to be held.

You are the in between
that finds peace in the darkness,
where beauty can be seen without sight.
You are the light that shines forgiveness,
my angel in the night.

Your absence is the weed
growing distance in my heart.

The lights come up and they
have all come out to honor you.
Do not fear the stage.
You already know how this one ends.
And when the curtain falls,
I will be the last one standing.
Standing for you.

You cannot tame that kind of wild
that runs with the light and darkness combined.
She'll swallow you whole and consume you alive.

> Be still
> my fate maker,
> for I have
> not begun to live.

I'll never be that glass that drinks away your pain .
I'll never be that drug, to shoot up in your veins.
I'll never be that high, you smoke to lose control.
I'll never be that adrenaline; you take to feel whole.
I will only be the love, that promises you to save.
I will only be the light, to help you find your way.
And if too pure to live in your world.
I will not stay.

> I promise,
> when it seems as if the world
> has left you behind,
> I will bring down all the stars
> from the sky, to prove...
> that the center of the universe is you.

I love you in the deepest way,
like a storm to cross the seas.
I would glide along your tidal waves
to bring you raging back to me

I may not be whole but take the rest of me.
Grasp everything that bends, ready to break away.
These bits do want to stay.
Take the messy, the melting,
the parts slipping through your fingers
until I rest in your hands.
Mold me back to beauty.
Make them see who I am.

There once was a man
who tortured my heart,
so I decided to torch him
from my soul.

Our love is beauty from afar,
but I will love you wherever you are.

Leaving you, leaving me, barely we were meant to be.
Sorrow borrowed, a new tomorrow.
Can you see, we set it free? It's fading fast, not meant to last.
Leaving you, leaving me, surely, we weren't meant to be.

My insides
have been torn down
so many times.
I don't need your arms
to hold me up.
Give me your
inner strength so
that I won't break.

Have I lost all chance of repeated time?
It stirs the worry in my mind.
Of minutes I have yet to grasp.
Mixing abruptly with my fading past.
No, I will not await my fleeting heart.
Impeding, no longer beating, do us apart.
May I worry not, as I still live.
May we live with all we have to give.

On the days that fill me like rain,
I let it spill down, covering the ground.
All of those city blocks
that we have ever walked.
I still fill to make way for you…

                          If a dream feels lost,
                          it is only lost if you
                          leave it in your mind.
                          Release it to the world
                          and see what it will find.

In the light, you are one of many
But, like faded stars across the sky
We need the night to really see us.

        I will never stop running from who I am,
          until I can catch up to who I am meant to be.
      I've left behind more and more the higher I climb.
    As the road disappeared, it cleared away those who
                    couldn't handle the stay
             Still, I will go, because I know,
                the end was always mine.

The water runs below and I can feel it in my soul.
Seeping, my heart is weeping,
taking away frozen pain,
melted by your touch.

If the blackbirds find my soul,
may they turn me into a crow.
Let them become the very thing
I know connects me to you.
Over flapping wings was the sound
of my heart breaking
the moment you let go.
I watched you fly away
clenching to my life source,
but it was mine that was dying.
May the blackbirds find my soul
and show my wilted wings
the way of the crow.

Give me the dark
and I will tear out the night
for the light.

      I want to relive you
         every day.

                I want to believe that
somewhere between the stars
and heavens that you exist.
For once there came a time
when you were mine. And
now I share you where
thoughts remain.

I don't need
someone to tell me
that I'm beautiful.
I need someone that
treats me with
beauty.

A frost adorns a once vibrant rose,
whose paleness sweeps the rouge from its inner pose.
Frozen intents, meant to shake this grace from its sight to hover near.
Its color may change, yet within remains its beauty ever clear.

I carry you in ways that were
meant to fade. Try as they may,
hands cannot erase the way you
exist in my abyss.

I just want to step
outside my body, so
that I can let go of
you.

Let me help heal you
and make you whole again.
I know what it's like to live broken.

Loving you would be
my greatest defeat,
because I'd lose
my heart completely.

I was born as fire burning through your flames.
Unable to tame, you are my everlasting fuel even after
you've burned out.

I will always find myself lying
In your arms, even when
There is nothing left to hold.
Give me reason to love and I
will give you all that I am.

No words resound, never rang so true.
My life would be nothing without you.

With every snowflake, I can
feel my heart melt as I fall
further from you. What would
I do to save you? For you have
already saved me?

Can I steal time
and make you mine?
I promise I won't settle
for anything less than you.

Sometimes
when words can't
find me,
poetry can.

It is not love, if it
has touched the
heart, until it has
crept in your
soul.

Love takes flight in the night, visiting all from a past,
now out of sight.
What encounters of care, for what is no longer there,
yet still grateful to find what has been left behind.
Wishing nothing but well, not to dwell on what wasn't
yours or mine.
Then I end with you. This is a different kind of reflection,
one that lost its direction.
Can I be careful not to bury all the weight that you still
carry in this heart?
This is not a visit, nay to lay you away. I am here to pay
tribute, to a heart that will never cease to end.
Still needing to mend, as my will you'll always bend.
Thankful for your love, because without it,
I could never have known how to feel this way.

I wander in this silence, unaware of this homestead.
There is a strangeness, that I can let go of a home.
Fields beneath my feet, they help me to be bold.
The steady that I know is on the road.

If I loved you, it would be written in
The skies of my eyes. This soul could
not hide the way it would write your
name on the plains of my very sight.
Would such power make me weak?
Can you be the last to know, how you
carry me so? Even as you transcend,
breaking barriers, I cannot pretend
you are not love. This would be my
very end...if I loved you.

I am yours when you are fading in the night.
And I am ours when you can no longer see the light.
When darkness sets in, do not give in.
I am always yours.

So quick to give up.
If you think that chasing dreams are tough,
then just remember.
You didn't want it bad enough.

One touch of your love
will last me a lifetime.

Before it is over and before it can begin.
I decided to love him.

      If you scratch away
        my surface, the
       deeper and deeper
       that you go, you
     will find me at your core.

Black sails hang over a sea pairing the night.
As I go, you could not have known I was a pawn in their plight.
Forced to walk the plank, I feel the splintered wood beneath my feet.
There comes a calm as they roar on against the end of loves defeat.
With surety and last breath, to face the ocean that I'll meet.
I may sink below, but you must know, for you my heart will still beat.

Do not forget me as you move on,
To those places not meant for me.
Starting a path that I'll never see,
You did not find me after I was gone.
I have faded in your dusk and dawn,
Never knowing for how long.
And you can easily let me be,
Have I no place in your memory?
I believed in you, us, but I was wrong.

        Maybe in another life,
    I was the one living for myself,
while you were the one dying for my love.

You are the random wild
Thorn bush that will bloom
the most beautiful roses from within.
A clever beauty worth waiting to pick.

    Why must this body fight me to sleep,
when all I want is to be left in your wake.

> When you fill your eyes with wonder,
> that love will lead you home.

I have never seen the moon shine,
the way it does behind those root beer eyes.
Maybe it's because you have finally seen the sun.

She was born in a summer among a snowfall.
A powder carefully crafted by her creator,
it did not melt the way she melted down those walls.
The winter would eventually take him,
but he'll exist inside the snow globe of her heart.

> I don't want to wade in shallow hearts,
> that leave me on their shore.
> Let me dive in a heart that's deep like the sea,
> sinking ships for me.

> I fear losing myself in a web,
> where only spiders exist.
> Let me live untangled and fly
> among butterflies…

Out of the ashes I will rise.
In these embers, there are
traces of weakness, the old.
My story has yet to be told.

> Beside the dawn
> of lifted days,
> there lives a
> sunset only we
> were made to cross.

> Stay strong in the storm.
> Sometimes you need to
> lose the boat to make it
> to the shore.

Let me pull you from the darkness. Help you escape
what you feel hides in your shadow.
There is nothing you must fear,
when I am near.

When my world goes dark,
send in the crows to pick at my soul.
Carry me to the other side,
shouldered on their wings as we glide.
Hear them caw together by the thousands,
skies turning black,
shaking the world with their call.
Take me to the one who gave
me these eyes when I was alive.
Only they know the way.

Let me blossom in your soul to keep me whole.
If left outside, I will wilt to stay alive.

I searched for safety in the things
I knew that couldn't give me shelter,
because I wanted to prove I was worth saving.

> Your love it crashed inside my soul
> like a raging stormy sea. There it
> swells, my insides quell as
> you sink me to my knees.

I have been touched by the wings of an angel
and felt the burning of the deepest sting.
Forever marked by your glory
and tainted by sin.

I am only insane because I am left with my mind
while you have left with my heart.

> Can you still live for me, even after you are gone?
> This life is mine, because of your existence
> and yet, without you, is there life?

> Falling into place,
> falling into you,
> falling into me.
> That is happiness.

> I would risk it all to have
> one chance to fall completely
> in your love.

> I never
> knew I
> needed
> you
> until
> you no
> longer
> needed me.

I have loved love over and over again,
blindly, steadily, without the promise of return.
I will fill those hearts full of lack, because I know one day,
love will love me back.

I knew when you held
me close and made the
world forget the
milestones stacked
against me. I knew
I wanted to be yours.

It was
beauties fear
to lose it and
a monsters
fear to
choose it.

How does the sun get over being
blocked out by the rain?
Such brilliant radiance shall never fail to shine,
yet in this moment, it gives way to thine.
The storm can last for hours, days.
In this way,
I too can feel you damaging my rays.
Tell me how to get over your storm?
As the sun still shines, surely, I can too.
I will get over you.

You are the fever
underneath my skin.
I am not waiting for you
to break. I would rather
you stay within.

Know that the best part of me
will always be living in you.

Only words will ever love you
more than I can, because each
word that I write is born to be
dedicated to you.

He may be hot for you tonight, but I am
the flame that keeps him warm inside
long after you have burned out.

In a world full of crayons,
whether it's red, yellow or blue.
I would pick to be any,
as long as it was next to you.

I do not want the flower that can only
bloom from my direct sunlight.
Give me a weed that can transcend
its roots, growing on its own.
I am safe in this strength.
Together, we will thrive.

Nothing breaks like the
sound of an iron heart.

I will strip away
your darkness and
blanket you in
stars.

There is no living, before ever
finding oneself. There is no dying,
before ever losing you.

Scorched like dragon's fire,
burning through my veins.
Like myths unveiled, your
love impales to prove it's
mine you claim.

You will not find me in the sunflower fields.
Though full of cheer, I did not grow from this acre.
Find me in the meadows, beyond the wildest trees.
I bloom through the winters and live for your breeze.

Never take for granted that a
Butterfly has wings. It began on
the ground, but knew it was more.
We were born to soar.

>   Waiting for an
>   ending before it begins.
>   Why dare loves embrace
>   if it can't ever win?

He knew me like an open book.
And I was afraid to open up
to anyone.
Hands touching me, I was his
paper, waiting to be
written.

>   I am nothing more
>   than everything
>   I was meant to be.

Two hearts begging to be free.
Before it fades give it to me.
I want to feel it,
bit by bit,
Love me like you mean it.

The throne of shadows, bestowed a King, supported by souls that dare not let go. Their love fed his idol as they mourned this man who lived a long time ago. A crooked nose, and charcoal eyes peered beneath his crown. A ruler once in life was now forced to wait around. The shadows clung, but he waited still, to fulfill a promise he could not bring. The stars of life would use their light so their love could save their King.

I'm jealous of the rain the way
it soaks you in, covering your
skin. Every raindrop gets to
touch and yet it is you seeping
through my pores.

I chased road after road, but it didn't matter where I'd be. Every road that I'd take, would lead me back to me.

Lead me to your wild,
where I can grow to love you.

> You are dreams sweet envy,
> bestowed upon my very soul.
> Where sleep nor wake, cannot
> escape the visions that you hold.
> This I say, you are the way,
> I could fall in love with
> my eyes closed.

There are no oceans
that could hold the emotions
you have filled in me.
No sunrise that could burn
the way you have torched my soul.
The coldest ends of this earth,
could not freeze me the way
you have stunned me still.
All the value in this world
could never make me
give up this one.
Not one. Not all.

Place me on you, as if I were the
only thing you'd ever touch.
Even if I am something you
would not try on, once felt, you
could never deny the way we'd fit.

He planted love
inside her heart,
where it has
forgotten how to
grow.

Let me hide inside
your darkness for a while.
Sometimes living in the light just hurts.

She spent all of her time aiming for
the stars that she missed the
magical moments waiting at her feet.

I am leaving now. Leaving
you behind. And when I go
for now, know that you
will never be far from my
mind. I will say goodbye
to you my love, but am
leaving my heart this time.
Hold on to it as always,
forever and I promise you.
It will love you till I die.

Her lion's heart
could not be tamed
by all the lies in his
heart.

When you dream from deep within,
their screams get louder for you to
fail. That is when you know you are
close. Fear them less as you prevail.

The goodbyes get easy,
with every piece of me.
Every piece that you have
taken, less and less is
breaking.

Doesn't it ever get old?
Their monotony wears me
like the stories they have
told. I want something real.
Give me something real to
hold.

I am not of earth or stone,
but a being meant to live in this space.
I would rather get lost in the unknown,
than lose myself in one place.

You are everything
I never knew I deserved.
A poets dream for love.
The reason for my words.

Your true test of strength
is not how you shine in
the light but the way you
glow in the darkness.

I cannot
compete with
all your
firsts or
memories in
your past.
But darling,
I would rather
be the one,
that you seek
to be your
last.

She wasn't meant for
yesterdays. She was
meant for the today's,
tomorrow's and
forever.

No emotion can measure or amount to the
way that I treasure the very existence that is you.
I know this to be true. Lost in your endeavor,
I will forever be the greatest love you ever knew.

          I'm just a rose,
          wilting for your
          love.

     Oh Valentine, you are divine,
     wrapped inside my head.
     Red lip-stained kisses,
     left like candy in your bed.

In the midst of all the chaos,
I am untouched by the reminiscence.
Untouched, because I am fully covered in the way I feel
for you.

Find yourself to
find your dreams.

When they leave
you let them go.
Better will not
enter, with the
weight that they
bestow.

The great battle of,
loving someone who can't love,
lies within your heart.

To be loved by a poet means
that you will be penned to the
world, the way no one else has
ever seen you before. We want
nothing more than to read you
over and over again.

Decades spent burning
through time like it was mine.
Wasn't it mine?
New tales told, leaving the old,
somewhere in the past.
Watching it dwindle, fading
ever so fast. Make it last for
your sake. It is not too late..
make it last.

>Lead me to the
Broken, so that
together, our
fragmented pieces
combined, will makes us
whole once again.

Embrace yourself and all
your wrong.
I never felt more out of
place, pretending to
belong.

They say that love is
blind, but I never saw
the world or felt, before
I knew your eyes.

You always had a way to make darkness shine. The way that
nothing else mattered, when you were mine.
I can see you in its feathers when they fly.
Watching me below through their eyes.

We will never find a cure for
love. We will only find the one
to numb its pain.

Can we fade beyond
the pale moonlight?
So I may see the way
that she gleams.
Off your incandescent
face in the night.
Unveiling the man of
my dreams.

Love is but a story,
painted by those we
want to see us.

You are loves first kiss,
that melts my lips.

If knowing you is the
definition of love, then I
shall wish it so.
For I'd rather know
nothing else again, then to
ever let you go.

Like a beautiful petal,
that flows down in the rain.
I may drown in the river,
but won't wilt from the pain.

If I could tattoo my soul,
I would so that I can never
forget you.

Never fear letting go and seeing what
love brings. A bird was born to fly,
before it knew its wings.

I fell in love on the road, in a place where I came to be free.
She'll break your heart if you let her, but she's still an angel to me.
Feel the warmth of her touch, the thrill of the night.
You can't quite explain why it always feels right.
She'll call to your heart, where the bands come to play.
You can leave in a moment, but from her you can't stay.
Such a beauty to behold and get to see with your eyes.
Where only stars can be born that are not from the sky.
Her image is a magical facade.
She smells like roses in May.
Oh, how I love to be in love with the one called L.A.

Where darkness travels, be the light that
loses their way.

The more walls I break
down, how can it still
leave me here untouched?
Let me feel every block,
every stone, because without
them, I am already
crushed.

                Every drink that was stronger
                than the other, could not recover,
                my lost lover. Every man who
                wanted more, could not restore,
                me being yours.

        Can we freeze time
        somewhere between
        tomorrow and us?
        I'm ready to live
        in your moment.

> She was made for the storms
> without shelter. Nowhere to
> hide, but to survive.

> In this moment, on this day,
> when the sunlight fades and
> the moon makes way. When
> my spirit has risen,
> among the clouds I will lay.
> Remember all of me.
> Remember me this way.

Where am I now
that you have left me?
Where am I other than
completely lost without you.

> Remember to hover
> somewhere between the sky
> and the earth. High enough to
> reach the stars, but close
> enough to fear falling
> to the ground.

Don't think of me.
I would never live in careless minds.

I was born to live,
to live to feel your love,
your love till I die.

  Through dampened clouds that hug the sky,
    a sun waits to be felt again.
   The rays struggle to break free,
  with that promise we hold on to.
I could never understand how one could yearn so much,
    until I met the frozen.

I am afraid
of the things
that I cannot
feel, because
I want them
to be real.

───────

      This feeling unknown, can it be my own?
    The stillness of this frame, it once called home.
By way of you it left, to reside there in your chest.
           Now memories of heart pound,
           miss the way you'd make it sound.
              But the center of me knew,
              it would only beat for you.

───────

Like a rare gem,
hidden below the surface,
while you wait to be discovered,
I have already fallen for you unpolished.

───────

Of heaven and earth,
I will honor you until
nothing else exists.

───────

      Break my heart
    and I will create a
      masterpiece.

Where will your assets
be when you take your last breath?
What of material gains
when there is nothing left?
Will they want you still,
when there is nothing more to give?
Would you change it all to realize,
what it is to really live?

Those who
are deceitful
will always
be trying to
lead you to
their truths.
An unweighted
heart need
prove nothing
at all.

When the dust settles,
I want to know that every
footprint left an impression.

> I am yours in all your flight.
> Black as night. In a ruling flock,
> you rule my heart the same.
> Hovering high, until
> we meet again. Until then…

You are every seam in this
warm woolen scarf that has
wrapped me in you. I promise
to never take you off,
as long as you wear me the same.

> I take comfort in this storm,
> for I cannot bare the sounds of
> your silence.

The only fault in love is to dare to give it all
for hearts that know not how to fall.

Sometimes I don't want to
let go of the past.
Some things are meant to
last.

―――

When morning
breaks in a summers haste,
I'll be fading in
your night.

―――

What sweet toxins are left living in this mind?
They quarry as they animate,
plaguing pieces they may find.
Mixed emotions, stirred by hands,
of that touch one left behind.
It wears me like a haunting frame,
forever to be mine.

―――

Choose me like you
choose your favorite cup
of coffee each day.
Effortlessly.

Pack up the pieces and set out to find
the beauty that was left behind.
Staying here would be like
losing all we have gained.
I cannot live in a world where I change,
while they stay the same.

She was forever a wanderer
searching for the reason to make
her stay.

        The center of his heart was a universe
            she wanted to soar in.
            He was so much more
             than those before.

            It still stings to be
      just your fling, when you were
              everything.

His words are her
beauty and he captured
both so well.

I don't care who you are.
I only know you as the one.

      There are no limits to
      our star gazing, because
      together we make our
      wishes come true.

      Stuck between two worlds,
      but lost in yourself.
      How can I ever go home?
      There are no signs in this place
      to lead me
      to where I am meant to be.

Carry me,
because I don't want to walk
in these careless shoes.

A humble rise retains me in a sunless dawn.
Where lines did not exist for right and wrong.
Great ships were seized from freedoms seas.
And the waves alone,
had carried me home.
Of young I toiled for what should be mine.
Though years go by, I've earned my time.
Oh bring me glory, for what is to come.
With miles unbroken, I've already won.

I am thankful for,
the way life brought me to you,
that your love knew me.

What's past those
steps that you used to take?
I cannot find your existence,
left scattered to the wind, erased.
Your particles stripped
my soul in your air,
leaving me here in its
place.

Your ruthlessness was all they could see.
But your weakness belonged to me.

I am half shadows and half light.
Glowing within, never letting go of the bright.
But without the touch of your darkness,
I would melt in the night.

I want to pair with all
your secrets and melt
us down in to one.
Together we make false
perfection look
beautiful.

>   Moments may disappear,
>   but I will carry you for
>   life.

Like a Butterfly,
in order to change,
you must never stay the same.

You are the
perfect setting
for visions to
be realized.

>   You hold me like the sky holds the stars,
>   illuminated by your kiss.
>   I cannot see what you make me feel,
>   but I know that it exists.

She loved them because
even the darkest creatures
need to feel the light.

        Love me like gold.
    Not because I am precious,
but because I am purely made for you.

I never met
crazy until I
followed my
heart.

    I'd like to believe
that you are the lesson
  I am meant to learn.

     She will love you from
         the other side,
because to her, your love
    will always be alive.

Your very presence sets my soul on fire.
There is no shade dark enough to
hide me from your light.
How destroying to be
out of your sight.
I would rather
burn within you.
Burn within
to feel you again.

        I could not imagine a
        world without you,
        because then there would
        be no world.

I'm only who
I am if I can
be me.

        We put everything in
        this world behind,
        to share the greatest love
        you will ever find.

He held her like the sunrise.
Warm, safe and with the promise of
tomorrow.

Pain comes with a price
and believe me,
I will pay for it.

I could never feel the depths below my feet.
I just always knew that it was there.
That would never stop me from treading in the open waters,
calm and fierce, not afraid to care. Because my love could fill
this ocean and take me anywhere.

Even the flowers seem
to bloom for you.
Happiness will grow
to any height
to be in your light.

What a mess you
have made of me,
but oh I am a beautiful disaster.

There is a lifetime within me.
Mine and yours from long long ago.
Through time we will stay connected.
You are my fixed point like a lighthouse and I
am your light that will guide your way home.

To live. Truly live.
There is nothing more
prevalent than those
that we have shared
this life with and those
we would die for to
share once more.

Somewhere in the middle of
my shine I am blurred by your vision.
Remarkable to blend in to all that is you.
I will never fear losing myself in your reflection,
because this is the image of love.

Happiness is true.
If magic did not exist,
then neither would you.

      Release me to the wind like
      a balloon that has lost its string.
      Watch my bright beauty
      disappear from your site.
      You will not hear me when I pop.
      Only I carry this pain.

We laid awake as
our faces touched
and I knew it was the end.
When morning came,
it was not the same,
I would never see you again.

I shouldn't claim
to write poetry
because the poetry is
written in me.

You move this world, it doth protest
in your glory to be sung.
For in its rise of greatest sets,
no grander heart was won.

I've never needed
anything more in this life
the way I have needed you.

Can you love me wild
until the only restraints that I can bear
are that of your arms never letting me go.
I may act as if I don't need it.
But believe me, I need it so..

Forgive the scars that
adorn me from this fall.
I will land on my feet
because I am planted
firmly to you.

> How can I be
> this tired just
> waiting to wake
> up?

I plucked a flower from its great stem
pulling petals, I then began
he loves me, he loves me not
hoping to prove my inner thoughts
they dwindled away
my hearts dismay
he loves to
love me
not

Manhattan man. Manhattan man, will you hold my hand.
Forget about the city or the things you have planned.
These city streets can't see you the way that I can.
I see the dust in the walls, the millions shuffling the halls.
I see the glimmer in the lights, while others lose site.
I see the gum on the ground that they don't walk around.
Among the grey and the blue lies a city I never knew. Until I say you.
Manhattan man, Manhattan man won't you hold my hand?

Two hearts collided
and settled in to one.
They knew it was decided,
before they begun.

In the presence of such light,
thou has blinded my sight.
There is nothing more I see
than just you and me.

Afraid to love, afraid to lose.
In the end it was not for me to choose.
Years pair like eyes to help me see,
the bitter sweet fate that is meant for me...

Memories haunting,
taunting me to try and feel,
were you ever real?

Protect yourself and your heart
while there is still something left.
But leave the chiseled marks they gave you,
so you will never forget...

Nothing is sweeter than summers skin,
more romantic than winters breath,
humbler than a falls palette,
more alive than a spring rain.

You were everything I wanted,
blended up in a perfect glass of doubt.
Until I saw what you were made of,
so I spit you back out.

You took away my sense of want,
when you said that you were mine.
It was in those words,
you gave me love,
what I needed all this time.

I'd trade in my wings,
if it meant saving your soul,
just to see you whole.

This compass has worn out its way, there goes my
safety net.
But I've been down this road before, just never seen it yet.
Feet kicking up dirt, spinning in circles, dizzy enough to see
straight.
Teetering to steady off my running, am I already too late?
You can't be lost without a direction, but I know where I
want to be.
It's like the path I need to follow, is the only one I can't see..
Show me the way, even if it is me who craves to be in
control.
I've been down this road before, please help me free my
soul.

I hope that you
love me
forever.
From this life
to the next.
As long as
we never forget.

I used to think that there was
nothing of heaven and earth that
could remove your torch I carried.
Until one day I found,
that one who pulled me back to the ground,
then all of your lies were buried.

The stars called to you
as if they needed you most.
If only they knew.

Your touch lays on me
like hidden ashes.
I cannot deny its singe
because I wear it on my skin.
Know this is true.
I burn for you...

I am the light the shadows choose to guard,
for they know the sin I've lived in.

Be it fate that lead me down this road
or stubborn will to paths unknown.
I trudged through muck so thick,
I wore it like a ton of bricks.
I carried this weight well,
for I would not forgive me if I fell.
I walked until my feet changed,
accepting that they'd never be the same.
My path unclear, yet pulled me near.
A road converged, where there stood my reason,
for why I had to endure each season.
Be it fate that lead me down this road
or something more divine.
If I never walked to the unknown,
you would have been impossible to find.

Distracted by love.
Not a day goes by
where you don't melt in my eyes.

We danced through the sky,
hands high, with love in our eyes,
chasing fireflies.

I wanted to believe
that there was more.
Even when less and less
became effortless.

Endless, the love
that so fearlessly courses my veins.
Boundless, the edges
of my senses that you reign.
Timeless, the visions
you give me, remain.
Doubtless, the only
one that I need to attain.

You would want me to think of you,
have me keep you close in my mind.
Make me believe that one day
you would be mine.
Until one day I realized,
you just loved to waste my time.

Even on the coldest days, that seem to live to freeze my heart.
Like snow, I'd melt for the warmth of your ways,
so nothing could keep us apart.

I have never been
afraid to love before,
but then again,
my heart has never been shaken,
the way you have
rocked me to my core..

I followed him into darkness
and he left me there, testing
what he thought he knew.
That without him, I would fade.
But he didn't have a clue. From
his absence strength was
summoned, in emptiness I was
saved. Unafraid, rising out from
the darkness, finding one thing
to be true. It was his shadow I
outgrew.

Dare I say stunning,
you are the most becoming,
phantom of my world.

       That feeling that
     happens before laughter,
or the lingered rush after loves first kiss.
You are a touch which is felt long after.
   The definition of eternal bliss.

I never knew
how to hold on to the good.
It never felt right in the way that it should.

   Little grey, passing through the light.
      Taking form out of the night.
Soft hearts whisper, they meant not take you from this day.
Your shade is luminescent, between the colors that you lay.
        Loving you this way.
Nothing shone brighter, than the heart of little grey.

It is not my time.
I may be out of place, but not out of my mind.
There are sights my eyes have yet to behold.
Moments to hold on to, so much to unfold.
Fresh grass that my feet have not met.
The sounds of this world, I wish not to forget.
It is not my time.
I have so much to give.
If at all worth saving.
Let me live. Let me live.

In loves melody,
you are the music that fades,
where encores are made.

The hardest things in life to attain,
were the ones I sought to claim.
The things that were easy to hold,
I never wanted to turn to gold.

In this moment, love was found,
when thy face rested upon
the back of my neck.
The way your eyelashes met my skin.
Then nose and lips, I slowly came undone.
In this moment, love was found.
Your face against me
brought feelings never felt before.
I felt you breathe. I wanted more.
With breaths sweetest touch,
I confess you are the one.

What is this poison that
spills through my veins?
It makes me ill, taking
over the source of
beating in my heart.
Be still, let me forget this feeling.
If this be the sickness of love,
then I am dying..

He was ineffable
and I needed
him like the dawn.
The chance to
wake in his
day would be
the beginning of
my perfect ending.

This clothe envelops me but you're not there.
Sleeves protecting, hang long past my frail arms.
Its fabric contains you still, I feel it.
And you hold me without arms or body.
I want to disappear inside your threads.
Threads that bear your essence where fabric remain.
It is a desperate attempt to feel safe once again.
I am as lost as this jacket that hides in my closet.
Give him back to me.
Let me hear him once again.
But this night is silent and I am alone.
Hiding inside this suit for tonight.
Letting it find me a faint air of comfort.
Before I retire it back to memory.
That once wore my father's name.
Oh how I miss him.

> They saw you as they wanted,
> a creation to be feared, admired, chased.
> I saw you as the one that you are...
> and it was you who allowed me to only see that face.

> I thought that you were
> something but I
> was wrong.
> Something
> wouldn't make me
> feel like nothing.

My heart behaved madly,
bashing the inner walls of my chest.
I could hear it screaming at me from within,
never so loud, it launched me to the clouds.
I was taken by this primal beating inside.
The moment we met,
you unleashed it wild.

You have taken
my heart, but I
don't want it back
after it has loved
you.

    Over and over,
  I would die through endless lives
    to live one with you.

Raging shores, purple tides,
the color of divine.
The image of your face remains,
forever to be mine.

   What I wouldn't give to hear the words
   inside your heart that are meant for me.
    We poets think of a million ways
     to profess our love to one,
      but from that one,
     only need to hear it once.

She fell for him. She fell for him like the last leaf
that holds on just before the cold winter.
Slowly falling, watching herself let go of
everything she had.
She fell for it all..

Compassion is needed
in the hearts of all men.
To truly help those in need, is a
deed not of ourselves,
but for us all.

They said they wanted a storm.
To withstand any downpour even
if helpless to its powerful waves.
But if I gave them what they wanted.
Would they still think the same?
When your existence is leveled and this storm
has taken all but your name.
Would you want it all then?
Staying here, holding on to my pain.
Or letting go, leaving me with the blame.

Be brave like the moon,
for she wears darkness so well.

The things that never break
won't ever get to feel what it's like
to love with many pieces.

You have melted me like
hot molten lava. My heart
lay dormant until it felt
your touch. Now, nothing
can keep this love inside.
watch it burn me alive.

I cannot change the past,
or control the outcome of it all.
To attain and gain, from mistakes, refrain,
but not be afraid to fall.
I'll give myself the courage,
to not be afraid to find.
The happiness that I deserve,
in this world I'll make mine.

For in this sleeps embrace,
entwined lay face to face,
I fight to stay awake.
Am I already in a dream?
Of this presence unforeseen.
If it so, do not let me know,
I'd rather not go.
See, I can believe in this too.
It is real because of you.

We poets are bound,
bound to our minds you listen,
listen to our souls.

> I want you to become the flecks in my eyes,
> so that you may gaze upon yourself and see,
> why you have captivated me.

For there is no morrow
if thy love is fetched in borrow.

I feel the pieces inside crumbling.
Demolished thoughts, spiral words,
crushing nerves as they fall.
Scattered in abundance until nothing is whole.
My body, the shell of once was,
grasps for the remaining embers that settle in my feet.
They burn to the touch.
I have never been known to self implode..
and the pain, is too much to hold.

You have no
idea how hard
it is to live
like I am
anything but
yours.

I no longer feel the need
to please everyone.
I have bled too much and you
have watched me bleed out.
Now the ground is covered in my care.
Where are you now?
You aren't there.
You're not there.

The sun lives each day to brighten our way.
A strength that burns with every turn.
How tiresome it is to be endless.
When life gets us down, we must always
remember that no matter
how many times we may set.
Like the sun, we must rise again.

High above the ground, among a sea of windows
I have found what chance feels like.
It's doesn't matter what the other windows hold,
because behind this one, I am home.

I am unafraid,
when the darkness calls to me,
because he needs me.

Slip in to my solace.
Feed me to your soul.

If I am confined to be
in the depths of your mind,
then keep me there.
I could not bear
to be out
of your memory.
Just out of my mind,
out of mine.

There is nothing
more elegant than
the way you
wear that smile.
It fits me perfectly.

These words won't let
me sleep, until out of
my mind they creep.

My silence speaks out.
Not all words are meant for you.
Just every thought.

Disguised by your lies.
Changed by your ways.
I no longer am myself because
you have made me.
Now I must choose.
To lose myself or to lose you?

                    You took me seconds in to your eternity.
                                Minutes to your affection.
                                  Hours to your perpetuity.
                                  I have loved decidedly.
                                  You have taken indefinitely.

Wear me down like a river
smooths over a stone.
Caress me effortlessly, washing over
my exterior until I am yours.
I am transformed by your love.

> Why do you lie to that girl of July?
> She can run to the streets, but can't run from herself.
> Everything you gave her, she just put back on that shelf.
> She's a sunset girl, facing that westward wind.
> She'll fake it till she'll make it, even if she don't win.
> She's a star in her eye, that girl of July.

Sometimes I want to step
aside and let the darkness
slip inside.

> I fell to your grace
> when I fell for you.

In a world full of idols,
beauty and fame,
where comparison to image
is what we learn to pertain.
Will you notice me among this,
or on your outside am I to remain?
Waiting to be the one that you claim.
I imagine one day, you will love me the same.

The memories of your absence
march in my mind to battles lost.
Waging war against the past,
not leaving me to rest.
Nothing has ever been louder
than the sound of your emptiness.

Let thy self allow
true love to permit.
Let it move swiftly
before I omit.

Just cut me out like paper dolls
and hang me in the sun.
Let my fragile thin paper frame
be subject to the wind.
Take them as you may,
one by one until the last,
weathered,
tattered,
but surviving,
still hangs in the sun.
That is the one I am to become.

For you, my heart races,
but there is nothing worth rushing
when it comes to you.

The love that you want should
not be held by a line,
strong in your grasp,
but yet slips from his mind.
He that earns your heart,
you will come to find,
is the one who will want you
all of the time.

Whence seasons dream while summer sleeps.
The lilacs yearn and their petals weep.
Where frozen pray to be touched by heat.
Only a warm dense breeze can thy foe defeat.
No fall, nor spring can ease their grief.
From a winters spell that needs release.

I never wanted,
in the way that I needed,
to which I love you.

What lies beneath those treasured eyes?
Only thoughts of me, I hope.

You make
reality
better than
any dream.

She loved with an intensity,
like hot molten fire.
Melting kings and their sins with her desire.
How fair is love, when it burned them dry?
Fair enough, she would say, good love is hard to come by...

Her hearts survival
came from his fearless defeat.
She wore his honor.

What is reality, but our own.
I feel because I exist. I love
because I cannot resist.
My world is not shaken unless I am not living.

Seek to not just speak and do.
Show the world the real you.
Be kind to each other,
never live for another,
and let your promises always stay true.

Loving you is all that
I knew.

Whispers to the wind, carrying thoughts like a runaway train.
Tossing me around like a broken feather.
Getting high off the burn of your flame.

Your torch remains,
though our love was fleeting,
but oh how you still claim
this heart and its beating.

We are connected
to a bond that withstands time.
I'm yours, you are mine.

Ten rows high, windows to the sky.
A few blocks down, the gondola's island bound.
Parks to the West, there's a beating in my chest.
Take me for a ride to that Upper East side.
Diving in this New to the York and all that's you.

It felt like an eternity
living in your uncertainty.

Am I the one?
More than just some?
For all that it's worth, I am done.
Give me reason to doubt, there is none.
You should know, it's my heart you have one.

Sometimes to feel right you need
to do what is wrong.
Taking those steps, walking away,
waiting for those words, okay.
It will be okay.
Even if it won't be, let it be, cover me.
Leave me unexposed until the storm is over.
I have lived in their mistakes.
Let me make my own.

Some souls charge,
electrify as they collide.
It was in your silent intensity,
that I felt most alive.
You didn't need to say it.
I knew you felt it too...I knew.

What sweet delights
roll off thy tongue,
oh beauty to be sung.
To captivate
with every breath,
then bury in my lungs.

In our souls we wept,
while love evaporated,
till nothing was left.

You are the luck that shimmers over me like rain.
Washing away my once muddled heart drenched in pain.
You didn't find me at the end of a rainbow lined plain.
I was cut from the broken, but you loved me the same.
Maybe, we are both just a little insane.

Flash those eyes at me one more time
and I will make you mine.

You drive me in range, somewhere between
your impact and your target line.
Pace is set, timing's right.
No doubts, lights out.
On par.

His stare alone ignites waves flooding those who dare to touch.
Both moon and sun fight to gaze this man who never needed such.
Attention was not his praise.
But oh, his love meant so much.

Let me live so that I may taste such pleasure.
Let me love without bounds or measure.
Rise and not worry,
die with all glory,
and be the eternal flame
that you treasure.

In this time, my mind is fleeting,
forsake the hour and not the meeting.
Of present time, I am not of you.
Can you hear my heart inside your chest?
It's beating sounds and will not rest.
No other noise can ring so true.
Thoughts of love can be so nerving,
wonders soft, am I deserving?
Extending lines to hold reciprocation.
The idea of it does not seem real,
but in your touch, I still seek to feel.
To release, letting go, a self damnation.

Too good to be true,
a view that cannot measure,
to all that is you.

    One day you will understand.
That on the edge of prolonged sleep,
when you hear the angels weep,
I will rejoice in the deep
silence of their song
that carries me to you.

Of all the ruins,
in all the world,
you had to love mine.

I never wanted,
to be anything more,
than the light in your eyes.

If I could put you in a jar, to keep you near, not far,
I'd keep you long enough on hold, to watch your magic unfold.
Because there is nothing that I've known, that I could ever try and clone,
the way you make me feel, so if I can bottle what is real,
I'll store you and call it love.

Our Love is bound to the mist.
Melting mountains and meadows
with steam rising between
your warmth and my cold
thawing heart.

        You found me
  feathers black as night, fearless.
   You called out to me before
     disappearing in flight.
     I was not left tearless.

A vessel moving without its fuel.
Coasting, waiting to stop.
You reach for my brokenness,
repairing everything until I became alive.
I am new because of you.

   You move me like a Sedona sunrise.
    Slow, steady, then all at once.
Painting my horizon with the warmth of your soul…
       I need it like that.

You ignited my life.
Made me feel worth it.
That's when I knew. It had to be you.

> Make no mistake,
> I will seize and I will take,
> the moments you thought I'd break
> and leave you in your wake.

Let me wrap you around like the rubber band on your wrist.
Feel your pulse race to match mine.
Wearing me out like hot summer's rain. Breathless…

Listen. Listen to these words
that reside within my mind.
They mean to take my deepest
thoughts and leave for you to find.
I have done my best to shut them out,
but one by one they tell.
Only I alone am left to hold
the conjure of their spell.
One hundred days, forever changed,
and I am here to say.
I'll write to write and share my soul,
a poem every day.

A flower in bloom,
reminds me of our new love,
growing in beauty.

Your words trace me
like chalk, unveiling
every outline that
you hurt.

Take me back to that moment,
so that I can relive it every day.
Your eyes said more than words could even say.
In your gaze is where I'd like to stay,
because no one else has ever looked at me that way.

Of all the things
my eyes have seen,
the best by far is you.

I NEVER needed anyone to teach me how to run
with the sea or how to fly on the edge of their madness.
I NEVER wanted to be anyone other than me,
even if that path went through field blossoms of sadness.
I NEVER tasted the sweet devours to succeed,
before knowing how dust dried my palette.
I NEVER walked over gold lined melodies,
without dancing to crumbling ballads.
I'll NEVER take a shattered touch for granted,
I want to be moved every day that I live.
I'll NEVER let their visions change my heart to be slanted,
I will love with everything that I give.

I want to be
the rain on your skin,
so that you may let me in.

I didn't feel it stop.
The air that I breathe.
I didn't see you take.
My heart's beat as you leave.
I didn't know how long.
To find the strength that I'd need..
to feel anything once more.

Endless thoughts stirred, left awake,
it is you that fills my night.
When two souls collide,
leaving love in their wake,
each takes a piece of
their being with the other.
Now etched in me,
there is no way to remember
a life before you.

Am I perfect?
Perfectly impulsive,
adventurous and free.
Have I done everything in life the right way?
Not of this life or any other,
I am sure of it.
I do know,
that with every beat of my heart,
I have loved.
I do love.
I breathe love.
And that is what makes
everything worth it.

Invisible wounds,
if left unopened too long,
bleed down to the soul.

Steal pieces of myself
to travel down the
depths of your memory.
It may be safer on the coast,
but I would rather drown in
your thoughts than be
forgotten on this shore.

In the light of the darkness, she is there.
Shadows follow close drawn
to the light that was born
from a King of Ice.
From this cold place,
her essence is a torch,
her steps a rippling light,
while a beautiful cape of shadows
drape behind her glow.
She is safe because
the light guides her.
She is safe because his
shadows love her.

Romantic drifter.
He was a hot air balloon
making her heat rise.

        Pages were made to hold
        these words meant for you.
        Eyes were envisioned to
        keep your memory true.
        Each day that I'm with you
        is like living anew.

I have decided to miss you
most in the rain.
For they will not see my tears.

        I don't want to sting from your embrace.
        I just want you to melt my ice away...

I stood there on the cliffs of Moher,
waiting for you to return.
And in these seas of empty fog,
your presence in me burns.
He who sought to love,
but holds me not,
shall never know I care.
With every wave that roars the shore,
sounds drowning me in air.
Some part of me believes
that on the horizon you will be.
Heading over recognized waters,
here to rescue me.
I watch before my changing eyes,
through seasons passing and rising tides.
On the storm born cliffs where my heart resides.

Blind them in your light,
do not fade in their shade.
Even the darkness must
surrender to sunlight.

She laughed at the backside of impossible,
sun rays flickering across her face.
Wildness challenged her with all its fury
and she challenged it back,
daring anyone to stand in her way.

I see us in the rising sun,
where the weeping willow sways,
and the wild horses run.
I see us in a summer storm,
in the fog off the prairie,
and where new stars are born.
I see us in the hot desert sand,
the moonlight on the water,
and in the trees of this land.
In a wildfire furry
or a snow covered bliss.
I promise my love,
to always see us like this.

I'll let your kisses
tell me everything
that is wrong,
as we lay her in this hour,
tonight.
Because when the sun
comes up in the morning,
with you,
I don't want to be right.

Under the moon, we danced to songs only we could hear.
You held me close not afraid to be near.
Fingers on my back, I didn't care if they were rough.
We swayed side to side over waters they dare not touch.
Holding on to each other,
knowing we were more than enough.

See not the raging patterns of my soul.
It would be like saying I love you,
when I only have half a beat to give.
For the other part I cannot control.
It has decided for only one, to live.

Who are you who read my words?
Do you judge the ink that leaves my pen?
These letters spilling from my heart.
I write because these words cannot
live inside of me...

You are the one,
who makes me believe in love.
The one who makes my dreams vivid,
only you, that's because,
you have given me the power
to surrender to fate.
My eternal reason,
my everlasting soulmate.

Too often I have
searched.
Too often I have
found.
But in the end
it has only proven,
to you my
heart is bound.

Sonnet: Fragile My Love

A soft exterior, carefully placed
Hides that of a pit she has held inside
Invisibly bruised, how sweet she still tastes
Not of the best tree, yet blooms from her pride

Can you love thorns when they protect a rose?
Sometimes the cuts are worth holding beauty
Don't judge that of a thing you can't compose
Let care of her presence be your duty

Bestow the earth, there is nothing to give
That would measure to your unyielding love
The promise to mend all seasons that live
Lies within understanding thereof

The tides of your strength hold purposeful care
Polishing edges, exposing her bare

Always remember
that the best is yet to come.
You are meant for more.

If were my heart you wanted,
then you have succeeded.
Yours is the love,
I never knew that I needed.

                  I saw you in the shadows,
        heard the streets call out your name.
     Your face flashed beyond the windows,
       held you perfectly behind each frame.
The wind carries you in flight with the crows,
  the puddles take my sorrow down the drain.
      City lights flicker as the wind blows,
your tickets punched to board the midnight train.
                 I saw you in the shadows,
       heard the streets call out your name.
      You left me standing in the boroughs,
        and I will never be the same.

    Sea-filled streets staring past blank faces.
       They know nothing of who I am.
     Sharing in space, but not my existence.
Your hand brushes mine, bringing color to this crowd.
  With just one look, I am alive in your eyes.

You chiseled at my exterior.
Not carefully, but slowly chipping away,
letting the pieces fall where they may.
Can you see the pieces you have made?
You created new art of myself,
leaving me unfinished.
Afraid of what I had become,
I took pause to my reflection.
I am not sure they will ever fit back together,
these new pieces.
But I realized I didn't want them to.
I decided to create a better version
of myself that only I would craft.
There would be no more of your mess.
For that I am now priceless.

What of the broken?
I would defend to the end,
to find strength again.

    Your heartbeat echoes, serenading my soul.
    I listen to the melody, letting it take control.
    Only love can sound like this.

I hope that you find yourself.
The breeze rustled the curtains carrying questions like careless whispers.
I hope that you find yourself, wherever you are.
The sound of the clock's ticking grew louder with every empty minute.
Storming this world to self-sabotage, you search for something.
I hope that you find yourself.
Is there a chance then that you will find me?

I want to fly with the birds.
Feel the breeze upon my face.
Chase the horizon to the unknown.
There is freedom among the clouds and this grace.
Let me trade arms for your wings even for a day.
I'll fly further than you've ever flown, this heart guiding my way.

Music is the gateway
to our souls.
Play my song and you
will find me there.

You've taught my heart well.
I knew nothing of this love
before there was you.

        It was their love combined,
              that made
           beauty divine.

If I have fallen,
I'll fall again and again
if you catch me still.

Forget me not, even after you've moved on,
when the memories fade, and the feelings are gone.
Keep a part of me that will never be erased,
because the love that we shared, cannot be replaced.

          The things I value,
      no longer measure objects,
        but of life itself.

> Below the surface, your face began to blur.
> All that was left was the image you portrayed.
> I did my best to see you as you were.
> Now I could only see you.

We have locks for a reason,
there are things we want hidden,
from the world or ourselves or the untold forbidden.
A guardian to hold, a keeper to hide, the lock that contains only knows what's inside.
Imagine a world with no lock or key, no secrets to hide, you get what you see.
As you peer in this keyhole, imagine what's there.
It may contain what you want, or that you can't bear.

> You are everywhere, even when you are not.
> I see you in all that you do.
> I feel you in all that I am.
> Your existence has replaced my own.
> I no longer need this heart, because I carry it for you.
> Residing in your realm,
> my heaven knows one name,
> that is yours.
> And your love will follow me even
> after I am gone.

A shadow of doubt with a weakness to spare.
The clearest realization for the strongest affair.
With feelings so bold, the need to comply.
The love felt between, too strong to deny.

You are the breath
that escapes me leaving
an air of devotion in my wake.
I inhale again, your scent
swallowing me whole.
You rip through my lungs
to claim this heart.

I'm drowning in your love,
pouring in, sinking to my core.
Bound tight by the shackles you have made,
you cast me off, then watched me from the shore.
The bitterness began to enter,
bringing in harsh truths not even the sea could wash away.
I tried my best to fight it,
but this anchor would not sway.

If you take all your pain,
with the hopes you may gain,
that uncertain fame,
will it lead you to what you think you need,
in order to succeed,
when that's all you believe.
Will you need to keep proving,
as the things you are choosing,
could be things not worth losing.
Will it set yourself free,
if it were all meant to be,
will it ever make you truly happy?

Her greatest prize
was to be loved in his
eyes.

Sometimes I run from myself.
Sometimes I let you in.
Then I run again.
From everyone...
and paint the roads with perfect disaster.

Sonet 6: Impossible

Like a flower that blooms in the winter
Or as one force that is unstoppable
How that mighty oak will never splinter
I will love you like the impossible

When a volcano spills freezing over
And the ocean settles down to a dust
From out of the concrete sprouts a clover
To love you impossibly, I must

Like a wildfire that's never been burned
Or if stars left their nights to live a day
As the sands of time cannot be returned
Impossible, I will love you this way

You are my only thing that is plausible
Still, I'll love you like the impossible

Walking hand in hand,
I will never let you fall,
my strength comes from you.

Why can't my love carry you, as it holds me every day?
Am I to remain your distant thought,
the kind where I just exist but never fade nor evolve?
Because I don't want to reside somewhere
between your past and your present.

She was his controversial love.
Both light and darkness wore her like a shadow.
A beautiful mess like a tattered dress.
The kind of brave that you wanted to save.
The kind of love he never knew he needed.

Endeavors lost, the time grows near,
all thoughts of you, I will hold dear.
In your absence, the toll has broken,
my heart no longer fully open.
The guarded stand, to watch me still,
but they don't see, you bend my will.
I love you now,
as I had loved you then,
and I'll love you till we meet again.

Live for each new day.
Embrace the past and present.
We are the future.

Being together
feeds my soul and makes me whole.
Let's stay in this way.

>You are the gold
>touching the horizon
>that makes the sun
>glow with envy.

She grew to love him like the trees of this earth.
The tallest nor strongest could not compare.
She loved his surface and everything beneath it.
His branches shielded her from storms.
His roots supported her as he raised her high above.
Made her feel at home like a bird and allowed her to fly.

As I retire for the night, with attempts to chase this day from sight,
my thoughts and mind begin to fight, to keep me from a peaceful slumber.
I lay there and I toss and turn, to fall asleep is what I yearn,
but the hours pass with great concern, I imagine this nightmare from days before.
Leave me to my sleep I plead, you have no idea how much I need,
it mocks me at my attempts to succeed, of having any sort of dreams.
And in these dreams, I cannot shake, my restless mind will not awake,
it seems this hour will not take, and I'll remain this fight to slumber
The hours pass, my mind still wanders, will I find sleep soon I ponder,
my thoughts of solace soon grow fonder, I can hear the sunrise breaking.
The darkness fading grows in haste, another night of sleep I waste,
that leaves me a new day to now face, in hopes that maybe I'll win this night.

Keep me close.
Keep me safe.
Keep me warm with your smile.
I think I'll stay in your winter.

For a moment I felt you in the here and now,
crossing over for me to treasure you once again.
Time stopped.
Help me to preserve your memory.
But the sands of time keep moving…
and just like that you were gone.

Wrap me in your laughter,
love and joy.
Gift me to yourself.
Open my heart as you open
my possibilities and my
dreams with your aspirations.
Each day with you is the only
present I'll ever need.

Your eternity
is placed upon the shallows
of my beating heart.

Do I compare you to sunshine?
Nothing has brightened me more than you.
Do I compare you to the ocean?
Those waters don't move me as you do.
Should I compare you to the stars?
No, wishes don't need to come from above.
Can I compare you to yesterday, today and tomorrow?
Because with you there will always be love.

When I met your gaze,
I just lost it in your eyes.
Never stop staring.

The greatest loves
are often realized
when they are no longer
meant for you.

I wonder how often your thoughts turn to me.
How bittersweet to be reminisced.
My heart will hold you each time it finds me.

Your essence lifts mine,
suspending my soul like fog
to linger through you.

I feel the heat rise.
Your empty promises burn,
taking your love back.

One day, you will reach for me
and find that emptiness you gave.
Because nothing stings quite like regret,
for a love you wouldn't save.

Sonnet: Nothing

Take this mind so that I can't remember
What sweet memories captivate my soul
Remove this heart that beats burning embers
Pulsating dust through my veins black as coal

Strip away your touch covering my skin
With it I'm weak, I would sooner be bare
Cut away this nose your scent lingers in
I would suffocate to not breathe your air

Replace my eyes with visions before you
I have learned how to live in the darkness
Shield me from hearing, give me words anew
It's easy to survive being heartless

When all's taken from me left suffering
Soul exposed, without you I am nothing

There are rare places,
that your distant love takes me,
but never to you.

>Simply put to words.
>You are my waking hour
>and my dying wish.

>We are both shadows of ourselves,
>connected by unfading love.
>You are the pain of my existence.
>I am the reminder of your life.

If words were lost,
be there no sound.
To thy beating heart,
I'd still be bound.
If time won't spare the depths of will,
this love alone would be there still.

>I am the fear under your skin.
>Afraid to be touched because
>you know you will feel.

Sonnet: What is Left to Love

These wretched things bid my heart such deceit
I clasp my hands seeking refuge again
In all honesty, whose fault for defeat?
But my own when I chose to pretend

Let me fly away with broken wings
Flying anywhere, further from here
Don't tether me close, we know what that brings
An emptiness you can't stand to be near

You've picked my bones bare, did you find me there?
No, I'm already ingested by you
Did consuming me mean that you still care?
Take more of me to find out that you do

Now that you are full off this rotted dove
Can you please tell me, what is left to love?

There has been nothing
that compares in existence
to all that is you.

Open up your heart,
among the mess and despair
you may find me there.

A crow calls in the distant fading light.
A familiar voice I long to hear...
watching over me waiting as I wait for you.
Wait for me.

I would learn how to
live in any life or die to
live another that gave
me one more moment
with you.

The rain is coming, but the flood still bares this land.
The sky it's calling, and the clouds fulfill its demand.
The darkness is rising, it leaves no pore untouched.
While the light slowly fading, fights more than enough.
The wildness is shaking, it's seeping through the sand.
The elements forsaken, for they do not understand.
Watch as it crumbles, you will not see it though.
This storm that killed this land, started long long ago.

To know you is love.
To hold you is happiness.
Of this I am certain.

There is no honor in loving without conviction.
Fear not the leading of your heart.
It knows exactly where to take you.

There are days when I feel you,
closer than before.
In time, I hope this feeling stays.
Memories were created
to hold you forever.

The sun at daybreak
warms me like your perfect smile.
I live for that dawn.

In the end it would only be you, gliding on the shores of my heart,
lost in the way you discovered it.
The irony of it all is it was once awakened by you,
setting forth this wave that filled my entire soul.
I fear the time, but still the beat is strong.
All my life it was only meant for you.
And sadly, when this emotion in my heart is swaying world's away,
slowly thinking it should be sinking, drowning,
it still fights the way most things would do,
unable to change a course this heart should be on,
very much aware of you still.
This soul, it recognizes yours,
forever changed by your eyes,
forever lost in your heart,
forever needing your soul.
And in the end, when I can fight it no longer,
when maybe time will have my sails,
in the end, it will only be you.

I search the stars for a glimpse of you.
If we are all made up of stardust,
surely you must be surpassing the
universe to find your way back to me.
I am not a quitter. You are the fighter.
Let's move heavens together.

Sonnet: Chasing you

These tempered hands hold moments that I've lost
Dancing over me with tiny gestures
Longing rushes through me like bitter frost
It's fleeting cold chills me beyond measure

I search for you without destination
While sorrow stacks forceful weight upon me
This will not be cause to my stagnation
You are far too crucial for me to see

But in my venture, I can feel you haste
It's as if finding you was never mine
Even knowing this I can't end my chase
All we seem to have between us is time

So I'll spend my life filling voids unseen
Till you I find, for my soul to redeem

There is so much more,
as there can be so much less.
For you I'm thankful.

Deep love was created by real love. This love, if ever felt, awakens the deepest corners of our souls and doesn't rise and set like the sun. It creates a permanent home.
Deep love reaches all your senses and holds feelings so strong your memories must always surrender to.
Deep love will always exist. But if not reciprocated, nourished or pursued it eventually is replaced by real love.
This love is everything it should be. Faithful, true and appreciated.
It fills your heart and soul with lifelong happiness.
But then why did real love create deep love?
Deep love was created because not every heart can feel it or find it for that matter. It is something so rare, that when truly felt,
becomes the greatest love and hurt you will ever face.
Real love needed deep love for a purpose.
To remind it what it lives for.

Today, like always,
I find my thoughts are of you,
and tomorrow still.

Sonnet: They loved

She loved him in that space between the veil
Suspended among a truth and sadness
Where pursuit only meant them to fail
Yet they continued on with the madness

He loved her in that space beyond his time
Another life where his fortune could tell
That losing this was the end of the line
And her heart would be the greatest farewell

They loved in the way that truly mattered
Just not enough to hold on to its plight
So like dust in the wind it has scattered
The pieces seeking each other in flight

They loved in a place that wasn't the same
Awaiting both hearts, where love never came

There are songs that play gently, sending love in to stormy seas.
You are not gentle. But this song wasn't written for you.
Yours are the lyrics I want to dance to.

Sonnet: Touched by the Sun

Like a fierce burning sun, your blaze finds me
It keeps me warm, yet shadowed by your guard
Time stands; I am the shore that meets your sea
Your depths, they pull me in, leaving me jarred

A darkness lives here, but I am unafraid
I sense your pain as it pulls me under
Drowning me in your desires and crusades
Is there a place for me here I wonder

You answer, lifting me above the deep
Arms clamping down, protecting who I am
You hold me there gently enough to keep
We lay side by side, the lion and the lamb

Breathing together till breath became one
Chemistry worth saving, touched by the sun

For every word that will go unsaid,
and with all the things we do instead.
For the chances we'd take, if we knew of its end,
or the choices we'd make if it didn't depend.
For the many days when we are not sure what to do,
and the many ways that things somehow pull through.
For finality, letting go, and moving on,
and learning what's right, can sometimes be wrong.
For what it's worth and the way things are meant to be,
and opening our eyes to that we should see.
For that which is done that we can never take back,
how the things that we need are the things that we lack.
For accepting the what, without knowing the why,
since every hello, must follow with a goodbye.
For living completely with this time, we have set,
every day to its fullest without having regrets.
For learning to love, even when it doesn't love you back in
return, by giving your heart up to those you've felt earned.
For seeking true love when it may have been there all along,
it may hit you so sudden, but already be gone.
From the confessions of my heart,
as our paths has once crossed.
I will never understand our love,
and the way it was lost.

I climbed into a bucket, that rested in this well,
and lowered myself down slowly, into the depths of
your hell.

In darkness I was covered, only blackness in site,
with each level I went down, saying goodbye to the light.
The bucket was cold, left me out in the open.
Exposing my fears, to what lurked in the broken.
It seemed like an eternity, until I felt you closing in.
I wasn't sure what I would see, inching closer to your sin.
The rope jolted to a stop, I swayed hitting the walls.
I clenched on to my bucket, not quite ready to fall.
Regaining my balance, I listened quietly for you,
for this presence I have needed, but now barely knew.
My heart thudded in my chest, but ached at the same time,
remembering those days, when you once had been mine.
It's like the darkness could see my thoughts and made way
for their king.
And suddenly you were there, your being my everything.
Your hair black as night, stood out from this dark well.
Your eyes sparkled still, in these depths where you dwell.
Tears filled my eyes, but before I could speak,
you reached out with your hand and wiped them away from
my cheek.
I leaned my face into your hand, unafraid anymore.
Finding your spirit, was all I hoped for.
Your eyes told me everything, how you hurt and your pain.
That a life lived without me, just wasn't the same.

No words were said between us, but the love was still there.
You took hold of the bucket and secured me with care.
He pointed above me and I understood then,
that our time together was beginning to end.
I don't want to go back, I want to stay here,
I miss you too much, it's you I need to be near.
He pointed again and I began to cry,
I don't want to leave you, please tell me why.
He kissed me on my forehead, gave one final stare.
Then the rope snapped me up and flung me back in the air.
I soared high above, letting out a heart stabbing wail.
I couldn't move or leap out of this small wooden pale.
And just like that, I was thrown landing on to the ground.
I jumped to my feet, the well nowhere to be found.
I stood there and cried, for the man who had died.
When he had died, he had taken me with him down
that well.
Now left alone, I must live in my hell.

Thank you for reading my poetry!

I hope that you were able to resonate with these thoughts of love, loss and pain.

We can find so much beauty inside when we can allow ourselves to grow where things had forgotten how to live. Much love to you...

Made in the USA
Columbia, SC
23 June 2023